It's All for The Kingdom

Why I am a Follower of Christ

D1416104

Tamekia Hubert

She looked back and marveled how far she had come.
She didn't wonder how she made it,
She already knew the answer. Only with God's help
had she powered through.
For without His strength, she could do nothing.

— Godfruits

Dedication

Thank you, Abba Father, for helping me to see that I am fearfully and wonderfully made. I am made in your image—I am your favorite, and I am yours:

"But you are a chosen generation, a royal priesthood, a holy nation, His own special people, that you may proclaim the praises of Him who called you out of darkness into His marvelous light;" 1 Peter 2:9

And to my love, before whom he departed, told me that I was chosen for such a time as this. Forever in my heart.

CONTENTS

Introduction

Throughout my life I've always been attracted to biblical practices and the deep things of God. Growing up, my friends would always tell me, "Tamekia, you are different". I would feel hurt because I wanted to be accepted and fit in with the crowd. Instead, I stood out like a sore thumb. I did not understand why God made me different. It seemed as though I was marching to my own drum. I felt that I was out on a limb all alone. As I continued to go to church, I participated in several different ministries: the prayer team, the hospitality ministry, the helps ministry, feeding the homeless, visiting the sick in hospitals and praying for their healing. I've always had a passion for God and to serve, yet with all of the ministries I served, I still felt empty inside. I felt as though I weren't fulfilling my purpose in life. So, I began to pray and ask God, what is my purpose? What is my calling? Why did you create me and what is my mission in life? As a result of my questions, God answered by leading me to enroll at Regent University, a private Christian school, to help in the discovery of my purpose. l enrolled into the School of Divinity, with my focus on Spiritual Formation, and l must say that my enrollment was the start of something great! l learned so much about myself that l truly can't begin to put it into words. One of my Professor's, Dr. Kristina L. Chalfin, gave me insight into the true meaning of spiritual formation and how conforming into the image of Christ takes a lifetime. Dr. Chalfin, thank you for letting me know that my calling is still being unfolded as l continue with my studies, and that it is okay that l did not initially know my calling. Just to know that alone has given me comfort and has been a huge weight lifted from my shoulders.

My first semester at Regent was a journey l'll never forget. Now that l was a student, l began to reflect and found myself drawing closer to God with each week that passed. l developed a deeper relationship with Christ and often found myself asking God, "what would you have me to do today"? l found myself praying more, meditating more, worshipping more, and setting time aside to hear from God. There was a difference. l noticed that in being intentional about my time with God, l was conforming into the image of his Son. I practiced these spiritual disciplines daily and over the weeks in the course, I allowed the Holy Spirit to examine me. The Lord began to reveal some areas in my life where I had not healed. He showed me that I was still holding onto unforgiveness, pride, and anger. These were areas in my life that had not been addressed. I had moved on and forgotten about it, yet still, I harbored these feelings. As events began to take place in my life, anger towards others would surface. I realized that I had not let God heal me and that I was still in bondage to my past. All of the hurt and pain, abandonment, and rejection, were still present. I can honestly say, that around weeks four and five of my spiritual formation class, I began feeling a little discouraged. I had allowed the Holy Spirit to examine me, but it was a painful process. Despite the pain, I suffered through and allowed the Holy Spirit to purge me. God was transforming me. God was changing me. I had become more of Him, and less of me.

I am grateful for the opportunity to study at such a fine University and Seminary where I can continue to grow and develop into whom God has called me to be. Even as I write this now, I am in tears. God lets me know constantly that He is near—walking and talking with me along this journey to ensure l reach the destiny He has predestined for me from the beginning. As l continue my studies at Regent my prayer is to continue to grow in my spiritual walk with God. My vision is to inspire, empower, and motivate women who are hurt, broken, rejected, and have given up on life. l desire to make an impact in the lives of those who've lost hope. l want to be the example that proves that you can overcome hurt and pain and life's disappointments, with the help of God. While l am conforming into the image of Christ may l do it with humility and integrity and one day be able to say that Regent University is where it all began.

Outside of my time at Regent, l've had many struggles. l've suffered loss, heartache, and pain. l know what it feels like to be abandoned. l know what it feels like to be rejected. lt is not easy. l can tell you from experience, what it feels like to lose a loved-one. lt is heartbreaking. l lost my husband to COVID-19, and there are no words to describe the magnitude of my pain. There are no words. l have to take each day as it comes. All l have to give, is one day at a time. But God has kept me. l am only here because of Him. He comforts me. He lets me know that l am not alone. He has never left me, and I know that He never will. I know that there are other women who have been where I've been. Women who have suffered loss, abandonment, rejection, hurt and pain. God's daughter, you are not alone. I've been where you've been, or perhaps, where you are. I've once walked in your shoes, and I know your pain. I want you to know that not all hope is lost. I want you to know that God is a healer. He will mend your broken heart. He will nurture your wounds. He will not leave you there, and certainly not for long. Just as I overcame, you can too! You will overcome and become all of what God has called you to be.

Why am I still here, after trials, tribulations, and affliction? Because God has great plans for me. Why have I remained a follower of Christ? Because through it all, He has kept me, sustained me, and provided for me. Yes, I've suffered. Yes, I've had to endure, but through it all, I am still standing. A survivor. A warrior. A humble servant and mighty warrior for Christ. I've suffered for the kingdom. I've endured loss for the kingdom. I have remained faithful to God, because of the kingdom. It's all for the kingdom—my suffering, my heartache, my loss, and my storms—because how else could I be a witness and testament to God's goodness, mercy, grace, and healing power? It's all for the kingdom.

"Though He slay me, yet will I trust Him. Even so, I will defend my own ways before Him."

— Job 13:15

Though I am suffering, I will trust Him. Though I do not understand, I will trust Him. Though I've shed some tears, I will trust Him. That's what the above passage is saying. Will you trust Him? Remember that God cares. Whatever you may be facing, there is nothing too hard for God. Your mountain may seem unmovable, but just one word from the Lord can change everything. Continue to put your trust in the Lord. He's got you. As you journey through the next few pages, it is my hope that you will become inspired, empowered, and motivated to push through. Push past the pain. Push past the fear. Push past the doubt, that says you aren't good enough, that says you cannot make it, that says you are out of time. You are good enough. You will make it. And, you are not out of time. Take it from me, you are not in this battle alone.

God is on your side. You're getting your strength back. You're getting your fight back. You are going to make it! With God, I know that you will.

Who's That Girl?

I've had to overcome many obstacles and stumbling blocks in my life. I have cried, paced the floor crying out to the Lord to help me along my journey and I am here today because He heard my cry and delivered me out of all my troubles. I call the Lord, Abba. Father. I am the daughter of a King, and my relationship with the Lord is personal and relational. Because I grew up without my biological mother or father, I learned of the Scripture:

"When my father and my mother forsake me, Then the Lord will take care of me."

— Psalms 27:10

God has been my Father, in the absence of mine, and for that I am grateful.

I must admit that I am still growing and learning and so is my relationship with the Lord. One of my challenges, is fear. At times I am fearful when I take on new projects, start a new job, or do public speaking.

"For God has not given us a spirit of fear, but of power and of love and of a sound mind."

— 2 Timothy 1:7

I've asked the Holy Spirit to help overcome fear, and He has done exactly that. Now, I am more confident, and if He did it for me, He'll do the same for you.

"I beseech you therefore, brethren, by the mercies of God, that you present your bodies a living sacrifice, holy, acceptable to God, which is your reasonable service."

— Romans 12:1

I believe God is calling me to a life of consecration so that I can impact lives and save souls for the kingdom of God. In my prayer time, God has revealed to me that I am chosen, set apart for such a time as this. My passions are praying, encouraging, and inspiring people to never give up when life seems too hard to bear. My calling to ministry and service includes intercession on behalf of others and servicing the needs of the brokenhearted, rejected, and outcast—telling them about Jesus Christ who alone can save and change their lives. I am on a mission for the Lord. I want to leave a mark in the earth that cannot be erased. I want to impact generations and generations to come for the saving of many souls for the kingdom of God. Spiritually, I want a closer relationship with the Lord. I want God to use me for His glory in the earth, as He has proclaimed in His word:

""Most assuredly, I say to you, he who believes in Me, the works that I do he will do also; and greater works than these he will do, because I go to My Father. And whatever you ask in My name, that I will do, that the Father may be glorified in the Son. If you ask anything in My name, I will do it."

—John 14:12-14

God has said, "greater works shall I do". I am just a willing vessel willing to be used for the kingdom of God. God has healed and made me whole. He's mended my broken heart. He's accepted me when I was rejected. He forgave my past and with Him I am made new! Who am I? I'm just a woman of God who has completely given her life over to Christ to be used for His glory. Who am I? I have committed myself to doing the work of the Lord. Who am I? I am a mighty warrior for the Lord. The One that died for my sins. The One that covered me when I didn't know that I was in danger. The One that restored my soul. He is Alpha and Omega, the beginning, and the end. He is Jehovah-Jireh, my provider. He is Jehovah-Nissi, my refuge. He is the Almighty God. There is none beside Him. There is no other like Him. So, who am I? The daughter of a King; grateful that the Lord chose me to be used for His glory. Grateful that the Lord has kept me in the palm of His hand. Grateful that He's blessed me. Grateful for all He has done. It is all for the kingdom. I am a kingdom warrior.

All for the Glory of God

The circumstances that led me to a saving knowledge of Christ began when I was twenty-nine years old. I went through a terrible divorce that left me without hope for my future. I was lost, broken, and ashamed that my marriage had failed. Here I was trying to build a life, a future, and start a family after graduating college, but life had others plans. My ex-husband and I were high school sweethearts. I thought we would grow old together, but he filed for a divorce, saying, "Marriage was not for him". My heart was literally ripped out while I was still breathing. I had to go back home to my grandparents, broken, hurt, and no identity without my marriage, so I thought. While back at my grandparents, as I was trying to piece my life back together, I learned of a Savior who died for me. He died so that I might live, who said in Jeremiah 29:11:

"For I know the thoughts that I think toward you, says the Lord, thoughts of peace and not of evil, to give you a future and a hope."

—Jeremiah 29:11

Although what I went through was painful, God pulled me through. I can look back and say, that it was all for the glory of God. My pain then is helping others now. I am able to say to other women, "you will overcome", because I overcame. Divorce is painful, and I can help navigate women to the path of wholeness because I have been there. Lastly, if they do not know Christ, I will point them into His direction, letting them know that He's done it for me, and He'll do the same for you.

1 Do it for the Kingdom

During the pandemic, I prayed and asked God to connect me with a faith community that would equip me for my God given assignment for the kingdom of God. God led me to Believers Faith Outreach Ministries. I saw them on YouTube and ever since I have been drawn to this ministry. I joined the church during the pandemic, and I am thankful that this is where the Lord placed me. Believers Faith Outreach Ministries seeks to develop warriors for the kingdom of God and to equip and empower believers to discover their fullest potential for the advancement of the kingdom of God. I was in the middle of transition and moving from one place to another. I was drawn to be a member of this church because my spirit connected with this ministry. I was in prayer, asking God what was my purpose, calling, and my ministry and He connected my spirit to this ministry. It was then that I was led to enroll at Regent University, into the School of Divinity Master's Program for Spiritual Formation. I gave God all the glory because He answered my prayers. I was seeking my calling when l enrolled at Regent University, and not only did He bless me to become a seminary student, but He divinely connected me with faith communities that could equip and empower me to be all God as created me to be. God took it a step further. He not only called me into ministry, but He provided the resources to help prepare me. He went beyond my expectations. This is why l do it for the kingdom. He surrounded me with Apostles, Prophets, Evangelists, Pastors, and Teachers who help equip believers to discover their full potential, all for the kingdom of God.

Why It's Important to Forgive

Throughout reflection, prayer, and study, I have discovered the importance of forgiveness:

"And be kind to one another, tenderhearted, forgiving one another, even as God in Christ forgave you."

—Ephesians 4:32

God brought to my attention many areas in my life where I needed to apply forgiveness. The brokenness, hurt and pain stemmed from being rejected and abandoned by my mother and father. I allowed God to bring these painful memories to the forefront so that I could deal with them and move forward on my journey to healing. I did not know that I was harboring unforgiveness. I thought, that if I had forgotten what my mom and dad had done to me, then I could go on in life and be happy. That was not the case. Every time my mom or dad came up in a topic or situation I would cry. I asked God, why He allowed this to happen to me? I asked God, why do my friends have a mom and dad, but I didn't? I did not even realize that I was harboring angry thoughts toward God. As I began to pray and ask God to forgive me for harboring unforgiveness in my heart, I began to feel a weight lifting off of me. I learned that forgiveness is a choice that one has to decide to do, and I am glad that I made up in my mind to forgive my mom and dad for rejecting and abandoning me so that I could be forgiven by God.

As I continued to reflect and pray about areas of unforgiveness, I realized that I was in bondage from my divorce in 2009. Although I had moved back in with my grandparents and moved on with my life, I was still in bondage. The divorce left me feeling broken, hurt, lost without any hope for my future, because I allowed my marriage to define me and give me identity. I did not realize that I had not dealt with these past issues, and that God needed to cleanse, heal, and set me free from the bondage of my past. As I continued to pray, God began to tell me that he loved me first and that I am the daughter of a King and that my marriage did not define me. God reminded me that He chose me and predestined me for greatness before I was even born. God said in His word,

"For I know the thoughts that I think toward you, says the Lord, thoughts of peace and not of evil, to give you a future and a hope."

—Jeremiah 29:11

God began to cleanse me and free me from the bondage of a failed divorce. Even though the divorce happened years ago, I was still in bondage because I had not renounced the lie of the enemy, that I believed my divorce affected my identity, when in fact, I had an identity in Christ long before I had gotten married. God still had a plan for my life even after the divorce. My God Jesus Christ has bought so much cleansing and healing from my past, just by studying, praying, and reflecting on God's Word and forgiving those who have sinned against me.

I have grown in ways I could not have done without the help of Jesus Christ and studying His Word and His standards of holiness for me. I am now encouraged to live a life of holiness unto the Lord realizing that my identity is found in Christ and not in people.

As I continued to reflect, I encountered in my reading, study, and prayer that in the past, I had been proud, selfish, and had a strong desire to do my own will. Before becoming a student at Regent, l was a perfectionist and needed everything to be the way l wanted it. l would go after things in life without consulting God. l would take on endeavors without praying about them and wonder in the end why it did not work out for me. l would rely on my own strengths and abilities and not the power of the Holy Spirit. l was more concerned about pleasing people as opposed to pleasing God. It was not until l died to my flesh and self that God could be glorified. l was tired of going in circles and things not working out for me. l was fed up with life and that is when l asked God to help me, to lead me and guide me. l told God l could not do this thing called life in my own strength and that l needed His help and the power of the Holy Spirit to come in and lead and guide me on the path that was set for me from the beginning. After asking God for help is when pleasing people was no longer an option for me. l was more concerned about pleasing God and the plan He had for my life. In order to continue to let God lead and guide me on my journey, l realized that l needed to maintain a strong prayer life, meditate on the Word of God, isolate myself when necessary to be able to hear God and allow Him to give me direction and instruction on the path and steps I should take to fulfill His will for my life.

I'm Still Standing

All my help comes from the Lord. I am dependent upon the Lord in all that I do because the Lord only knows my beginning and my end. As I look back over my life and marvel on how far I have come I give all the glory to God, because without God's help and His strength I could do nothing. God told me in His Word,

"But seek first the kingdom of God and His righteousness, and all these things shall be added to you."

– Matthew 6:33

I include God in everything that I do in life so that my desires and things will be added unto me. God has added unto me, peace, strength, and joy. Now when I encounter others who may reject me, I revert back to 1 Samuel 8:7:

"And the Lord said to Samuel, "Heed the voice of the people in all that they say to you; for they have not

rejected you, but they have rejected Me, that I should not reign over them."

— 1 Samuel 8:7

I must still be mindful and remember that I am a servant of God no matter who rejects, betrays, or disagrees with me. I will always bring my situation to God in prayer and allow Him to lead and guide me with how to handle it. Through it all, God has sustained me. Through brokenness, heartache, and pain, God has delivered me from them all. And because God has delivered me, I will continue to live for Him. I will follow Him, and I will serve Him, all the days of my life.

When I go to my eternal reward I want to be remembered as a humble servant of the Lord, a mighty warrior for Christ whose passion was to win souls for the kingdom of God. Because of Him I am still standing. God is not finished with me yet, and I know that my latter day will be greater than my former. All the glory and honor belong to Him.

Acknowledgements

To my late husband, Woonlee Hubert, who told me, "Honey, God has as a great plan for your life", and who inspired me to write. Rest in heaven my love, gone but not forgotten.

To my family: my mom, the late Josephine Butler, gone but not forgotten, and dad, my grandparents Richard and Frances Butler, my sisters Shakeshia Reid and Kenya Adelekan, my brothers-in-law, my brother, my auntie Pamela Butler, my uncle James Walker, my nieces Rachel and Abigail, my nephews, cousins, friends, and all the rare individuals in my life who listened without judgement, spoken without prejudice, helped me without entitlement, understood without pretension, and loved me without condition. Thank you each of you for your support; I am forever grateful. I love each and every one of you.

Special Thanks...

I'd like to especially thank Pastor Cecil Lamb and his beautiful wife, Mrs. Benza Lamb of Spirit of Christ Center and Ministries in Miami, Florida, where I was taught the word of God line upon line and precept upon precept. Thank you to all my church family there. Love you Larncy Rolle. A special thank you to One Body In Christ In Love Ministries in Miami, Florida, where I was taught how to be a soldier for Christ. Love you Apostle Darryl K. Auberry and your beautiful wife, Mrs. Tawanda Auberry. Thank you to all my church family there. Love you, Christina Lee. And lastly, I have to give a special thanks to my awesome, bold, beautiful, creative, and fearless nieces, Rachel and Abigail, who told me, "Auntie, open up your mouth and speak, just do it—no fear and never be afraid to bounce to the beat of your own drum". Auntie loves you both.

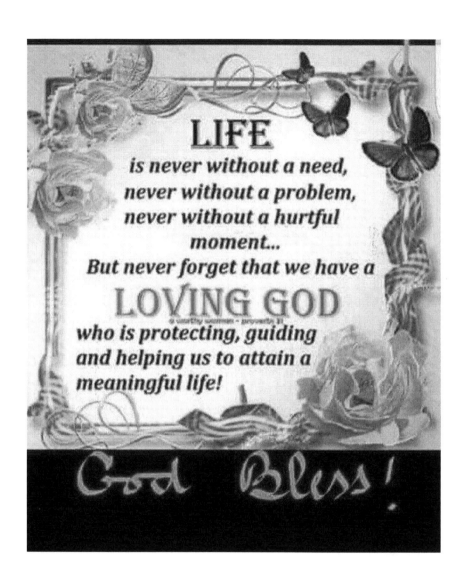

LIFE
is never without a need,
never without a problem,
never without a hurtful
moment...
But never forget that we have a
LOVING GOD
who is protecting, guiding
and helping us to attain a
meaningful life!

God Bless!

Made in the USA
Columbia, SC
15 April 2022